Bond

English

Assessment Papers

9–10 years
Book 1

**J M Bond and
Sarah Lindsay**

OXFORD
UNIVERSITY PRESS

Great Clarendon Street, Oxford, OX2 6DP, United Kingdom

Oxford University Press is a department of the University of Oxford. It furthers the University's objective of excellence in research, scholarship, and education by publishing worldwide. Oxford is a registered trade mark of Oxford University Press in the UK and in certain other countries

First published in 1973 by Thomas Nelson and Sons Ltd
This edition published in 2014

British Library Cataloguing in Publication Data
Data available

978-1-4085-2519-7

10 9 8 7 6 5 4

Printed in Great Britain by Ashford Colour Press Ltd

Acknowledgements

Page make-up by OKS Prepress, India
Illustrations by Nigel Kitching

We are grateful for permission to reprint extracts from the following copyright material:

P6 'Give Yourself a Hug' copyright © Grace Nichols 1994 reproduced with permission of Curtis Brown Group Ltd; p8 'A Week of Winter Weather' by Wes Magee reproduced by permission of the author; p27 'The Night Mail' by W H Auden from *Collected Poems* reproduced by permission of Faber and Faber Ltd; p33 'The Hyena and the Dead Ass' retold by Rene Guillot, from *The Children of the Wind* selected and translated by Gwen Marsh. Oxford University Press 1964, English translation copyright © Oxford University Press; p48 extract from *The BFG* by Roald Dahl published by Jonathan Cape Ltd & Penguin Books Ltd reprinted by permission of David Higham Associates and Farrar, Straus & Giroux Inc.; p53 extract from *The Hobbit* by J R R Tolkien © The J R R Tolkien Estate Limited 1937, 1965. Reproduced by permission of HarperCollins Publishers Ltd; p62 'The Sound Collector' by Roger McGough from *Pillow Talk* copyright © Roger McGough 1990. Reproduced by permission of Peters Fraser & Dunlop (www.petersfraserdunlop.com) and United Agents on behalf of Roger McGough.

Although we have made every effort to trace and contact all copyright holders before publication this has not been possible in all cases. If notified, the publisher will rectify any errors or omissions at the earliest opportunity.

Before you get started

What is Bond?

This book is part of the Bond Assessment Papers series for English, which provides **thorough and continuous practice of key English skills** from ages five to thirteen. Bond's English resources are ideal preparation for Key Stage 1 and Key Stage 2 SATs, the 11+ and other selective school entrance exams.

What does this book cover and how can it be used to prepare for exams?

English 9-10 Book 1 and *Book 2* can be used both for general practice and as part of the run up to 11+ exams, Key Stage 2 SATs and other selective exams. The papers practise comprehension, spelling, grammar and vocabulary work. The coverage is also matched to the National Curriculum and the National Literacy Strategy. It is outside the scope of this book to practise extended and creative writing skills. *Bond The secrets of Writing* provides full coverage of writing skills.

What does the book contain?

- **12 papers** – each one contains 100 questions.

- **Tutorial links throughout** – ⌷ – this icon appears in the margin next to the questions. It indicates links to the relevant section in *How to do ... 11+ English*, our invaluable subject guide that offers explanations and practice for all core question types.

- **Scoring devices** – there are score boxes in the margins and a Progress Chart on page 64. The chart is a visual and motivating way for children to see how they are doing. It also turns the score into a percentage that can help decide what to do next.

- **Next Steps Planner** – advice on what to do after finishing the papers can be found on the inside back cover.

- **Answers** – located in an easily-removed central pull-out section.

How can you use this book?

One of the great strengths of Bond Assessment Papers is their flexibility. They can be used at home, in school and by tutors to:

- set **timed formal practice** tests – allow about 45 minutes per paper. Reduce the suggested time limit by five minutes to practise working at speed.

- provide **bite-sized chunks** for regular practice

- highlight **strengths and weaknesses** in the core skills

- identify **individual needs**

- set **homework**

- follow a **complete 11+ preparation strategy** alongside *The Parents' Guide to the 11+* (see below).

It is best to start at the beginning and work though the papers in order. If you are using the book as part of a careful run-in to the 11+, we suggest that you also have four other essential Bond resources close at hand:

How to do ... 11+ English: the subject guide that explains all the question types practised in this book. Use the cross-reference icons to find the relevant sections.

The secrets of Comprehension: the practical handbook that clearly shows children how to read and understand the text, understand the questions and assess their own answers.

The secrets of Writing: the essential resource that explains the key components of successful writing.

The Parents' Guide to the 11+: the step-by-step guide to the whole 11+ experience. It clearly explains the 11+ process, provides guidance on how to assess children, helps you to set complete action plans for practice and explains how you can use *English 9-10 Book 1* and *Book 2* as part of a strategic run-in to the exam.

See the inside front cover for more details of these books.

What does a score mean and how can it be improved?

It is unfortunately impossible to predict how a child will perform when it comes to the 11+ (or similar) exam if they achieve a certain score on any practice book or paper. Success on the day depends on a host of factors, including the scores of the other children sitting the test. However, we can give some guidance on what a score indicates and how to improve it.

If children colour in the Progress Chart on page 64, this will give an idea of present performance in percentage terms. The Next Steps Planner inside the back cover will help you to decide what to do next to help a child progress. It is always valuable to go over wrong answers with children. If they are having trouble with any particular question type, follow the tutorial links to *How to do ... 11+ English* for step-by-step explanations and further practice.

Don't forget the website...!

Visit www.bond11plus.co.uk for lots of advice, information and suggestions on everything to do with Bond, the 11+ and helping children to do their best.

Key words

Some special words are used in this book. You will find them in **bold** each time they appear in the Papers. These words are explained here.

abbreviation	a word or words which are shortened
abstract noun	a word referring to a concept or idea *love*
acronym	a word or letter string made up from the initial letters of other words
adjectival phrase	a group of words describing a noun
adjective	a word that describes somebody or something
adverb	a word that gives extra meaning to a verb
alphabetical order	words arranged in the order found in the alphabet
antonym	a word with a meaning opposite to another word *hot – cold*
clause	a section of a sentence with a verb
collective noun	a word referring to a group *swarm*
compound word	a word made up of two other words *football*
conjunction	a word used to link sentences, phrases or words *and, but*
connective	a word or words that join clauses or sentences
contraction	two words shortened into one with an apostrophe placed where the letter/s have been dropped *do not = don't*
definition	a meaning of a word
dialect	regional variation of vocabulary in the spoken language
diminutive	a word implying smallness *booklet*
future tense	form of a verb showing something that will or may happen
homophone	a word that has the same sound as another but a different meaning or spelling *right/write*
metaphor	an expression in which something is described in terms usually associated with another *the sky is a <u>sapphire</u> sea*
modal verb	a verb that changes the meaning of other verbs, for example can, will
noun	a word for somebody or something
onomatopoeic	a word that echoes a sound associated with its meaning *hiss*
parenthesis	this is a word or phrase that is separated off from the main sentence by brackets, commas or dashes usually because it contains additional information not essential to its understanding
past tense	form of a verb showing something that has already happened
personal pronoun	a pronoun used when writing about ourselves *I, you*
phrase	a group of words that act as a unit
plural	more than one *cats*
possessive pronoun	a pronoun showing to whom something belongs *mine, ours, his, hers, yours, theirs*
prefix	a group of letters added to the beginning of a word *un, dis*
preposition	a word that relates other words to each other – *he sat <u>behind</u> me, the book <u>on</u> the table*
present tense	form of a verb showing something happening now
pronoun	a word used to replace a noun
proper noun	the names of people, places etc. *Ben*
relative clause	a special type of clause that makes the meaning of a noun more specific, for example The prize *that I won* was a book
reported speech	what has been said, without using the exact words or speech marks
root word	a word to which prefixes or suffixes can be added to make another word *<u>quick</u>ly*
singular	one *cat*
suffix	a group of letters added to the end of a word *ly, ful*
synonym	a word with the same or very similar meaning to another word *quick – fast*
verb	a 'doing' or 'being' word

This is part of an old recipe to make rock cakes.

After you have spread the clean cooking cloth on the table, you must get together the ingredients. You will want:

6 ounces flour
2 ounces currants
1 egg
2 ounces butter   *5*
3 ounces castor sugar
1 teaspoon baking powder
$\frac{1}{2}$ teaspoon ground ginger
1 dessert spoonful milk   *10*

If you have any nice Beef Dripping you can use that instead of the butter, or you could use margarine, but butter is best.

Weigh the ingredients on the kitchen scales, and be careful to see that you have just the right quantity of everything.

Getting the oven ready   *15*

Now you had better light your oven gas, as you will want it hot by the time the cakes are ready to go in. (If you are cooking by a kitchen range, you will not have to do this, as your oven will be already getting hot, I expect.) Don't turn on the tap until you have got your matches in your hand, as we don't want the gas to escape. Open the door, turn on the tap, and light the rows of jets, gently, and close the door again.   *20*

Cleaning the currants

Then clean your currants. This is the best way. Put them into a basin with tepid water, and wash them. Pour the water away through a colander, so as not to pour away the currants and, with fresh water, give them a second wash. Pour this away, and rub the currants in a clean cloth. After that, put them into the oven on a plate   *25* for a few minutes, to finish drying. You don't want the oven hot for this, as you do not want the currants cooked yet. So if you have been very quick about them, and you put the plate on a low shelf, which is cooler than the top of the oven, that will probably be just right.

If the oven has got hot before your currants are ready, you must turn the gas very   *30* low while they are drying. They must be quite dry, without being cooked. The reason you have to be so particular is that your cakes will be more likely to be heavy if you do not put the fruit in quite dry.

Once the currants are dry take them out and pick them. By that I mean, take the stalks off. Some will have come off when you rubbed the currants in the cloth.   *35*

Mixing and beating

Put the flour into the bowl, with the baking powder, and mix well with a wooden
spoon. Next, holding the butter between the thumb and first finger of your left hand,
shred it – or cut it into thin slices – and let it drop into the flour. With the tips of your
fingers rub the butter into the flour. Keep on working it about with your fingers   *40*
until there are no lumps at all, but the mixture feels like breadcrumbs. Now add the
sugar, currants and ginger, and mix all well together.

Beat up your egg with an egg whisk or a fork, or some people use a knife, until it is
frothy. Add this to the mixture and beat well. Put the milk into the cup in which you
have beaten the egg – so as not to waste any of the egg – and then add that to the   *45*
basin. Keep on beating until all the ingredients are well mixed. The mixture should be
quite stiff, and not at all liquid.

Underline the correct answers.

   1 (Margarine, Butter, Beef dripping) is best to use when making rock cakes.

   2 What might escape if the tap is turned on too soon? (water, gas, air)

   3 (Sugar and flour, Sugar and ginger, Baking powder and sugar) are added to the
     fat and flour mixture with the currants.

             (3)

Answer these questions.

   4 The author describes in detail why it is so important for the currants to be dry.

     What do you think the word 'heavy' (line 33) means in this context?

     _____

   5–6 Copy two examples from the passage that show this recipe was written nearly
       100 years ago.

       _____

       _____

   7–10 Rewrite the 'Cleaning the currants' section as simply as possible in four steps.

       _____

       _____

       _____

       _____

             (7)

Underline the correct **homophone** in each bracket.

11–12 The (scent, sent) of the flowers you (scent, sent) me is strong.

13–14 Tom (threw, through) the ball (threw, through) the window.

15–16 The (not, knot) joining these ropes is (not, knot) tied tightly.

17–18 Michelle cut her hand on the (pain, pane) of glass and she was in great (pain, pane).

19–20 I saw him (stair, stare) at the man on the (stairs, stares).

E 2
10

Circle the silent letter in each of these words.

E 2

21 cupboard   **22** wreckage

23 budget   **24** switch

25 thumbnail   **26** column

6

Add the missing commas to these sentences.

D 4

27–29 Sam loved going for walks swimming in the duck pond chasing rabbits chewing a bone and sleeping in front of the fire.

30–31 The baby cries when it is tired hungry has a tummy ache or has a dirty nappy.

32–34 Jack wanted a new bike some colouring pens a computer game new trainers and a pet dog for his birthday!

8

Circle the **nouns**.

D 6

35–41 gatepost   fetched   York   Monday

bunch   banana   under   frighten

fought   violin   team   sunny

7

Choose an **adverb** to fill each gap. Each **adverb** may be used only once.

D 6

suddenly   neatly   heavily   soundly

smartly   greedily   swiftly

42 Kim _____ wrote a letter.

43 The old tramp _____ ate his food.

44 All day the rain fell _____.

45 The child slept _____.

46 The boy ran _____ in the race.

47 The car braked _____.

48 The young woman always dressed _____.

Write the **plural** form of each of these **nouns**.

49 telephone _____

50 thief _____

51 museum _____

52 church _____

53 tragedy _____

54 roof _____

Add the missing punctuation at the end of each sentence.

55 Watch out, James is coming_____

56 Many people had left their homes_____

57 It must be time to have dinner_____

58 Where has your Grandad gone_____

59 Why do I have to brush my teeth every day_____

60 The snow dropped silently, covering the ground_____

61 Quick, the film is about to start_____

Rewrite these sentences changing them from **plural** to **singular**.

62–64 The girls ran to catch their buses.

_____

65–66 They had collected money to give to the homeless children.

_____

67–69 The lambs bounced towards their mothers.

_____

Underline the **pronouns** in the following passage.

70–75 We are going to Hull to see the docks. We will see several ships and if we are lucky they might let us look around them.

Underline one word in each group which is *not* a **synonym** for the rest.

76 hold	maintain	keep	destroy	retain
77 beautiful	nasty	lovely	pretty	handsome
78 happy	unwell	sick	ill	unhealthy
79 disagree	willing	differ	opposite	dissent
80 unhappy	sad	gloomy	upset	delighted
81 gigantic	enormous	big	tiny	large

6

Give Yourself a Hug

Give yourself a hug
when you feel unloved

Give yourself a hug
when people put on airs
to make you feel a bug   5

Give yourself a hug
when everyone seems to give you
a cold-shoulder shrug

Give yourself a hug –
a big big hug   10

And keep on singing
'Only one in a million like me
Only one in a million-billion-trillion-zillion
like me.'

by Grace Nichols

Answer these questions.

82 Which line in the poem repeats itself four times? _____

83–84 Write two reasons listed in the poem, why you should 'give yourself a hug'.

_____

_____

85 What is the meaning of 'a cold-shoulder shrug' on line 8 of the poem?

_____

86–87 What point is the poet making in the final verse? Use evidence from this verse to support your answer.

_____

_____

6

Write each of these words as an **adjective** by adding the **suffix** *ful*.

88 care   _____

89 duty   _____

90 plenty   _____

91 beauty   _____

92 wonder   _____

Copy each of these **phrases** making each **singular noun** plural.

Don't forget to add the missing apostrophe.

93–94 the three dog collars   _____

95–96 the two cinema screens   _____

97–98 the three boy books   _____

99–100 the two house chimneys   _____

Now go to the Progress Chart to record your score!   Total   100

A Week of Winter Weather

On Monday icy rain poured down
and flooded drains all over town.
Tuesday's gales bashed elm and ash;
dead branches came down with a crash.
On Wednesday bursts of hail and sleet,   5
no-one walked along the street.
Thursday stood out clear and calm
but the sun was paler than my arm.
Friday's frost that bit your ears
was cold enough to freeze your tears.   10
Saturday's sky was ghostly grey;
we smashed ice on the lake today.
Christmas Eve was Sunday ... and
snow fell and fell across the land.

by Wes Magee

Underline the correct answers.

1 On which day was there flooding?

(Monday, Wednesday, Friday)

2 On which day were we told there was no wind?

(Wednesday, Thursday, Saturday)

3 Which day of the week was Christmas Day?

(Sunday, Monday, Tuesday)

Answer these questions.

4–5 Pick out the two lines which describe the effect the weather has on the trees.

_____

_____

6–8 Write a word in the poem that rhymes with each of the following words.

calm _____   and _____   grey _____

9–10 The first two lines of the poem describe rain on a winter's day.

Rewrite these two lines describing rain on a summer's day.

_____

_____

Find seven different **verbs** in the poem 'A Week of Winter Weather' by Wes Magee.

11–17 _____   _____   _____

_____   _____   _____

_____

Underline one **clause** in each of these sentences.

18 The goats pushed their way out of their pen because they had spotted some apples.

19 The cars raced past us while we waited at the side of the motorway.

20 Matthew's present was quickly hidden under the sofa as he came in through the door.

21 Some children wanted to go swimming even though the water was freezing.

22 The hat fitted perfectly but it was the wrong colour.

23 It started to rain heavily as darkness fell over the sleepy village.

Underline the **root word** for each of these words.

24 unhappy   **25** jumped   **26** quickly

27 displacement   **28** uncertain   **29** affix

30 untie   **31** stronger   **32** mistrusted

Match a word with the same letter string but a different pronunciation, to each of these words.

height   foot   have   cough

drought   both   move   flower

33 bough   _____   **34** weight   _____

35 boot   _____   **36** cave   _____

37 moth   _____   **38** love   _____

39 slower   _____   **40** thought   _____

7

D 6

7

D 2

6

E 2

9

E 2

8

Copy these sentences and write a **possessive pronoun** in place of the words in bold.

41–42 **Your hair** looks longer than **my hair.** _____

43–44 **Our house** is smaller than **David's house.** _____

45–46 **Their dog** runs faster than **our dog.** _____

Write the masculine of each of the following words.

47 waitress _____ 48 aunt _____

49 queen _____ 50 niece _____

51 woman _____ 52 cow _____

53 vixen _____ 54 duchess _____

Add the missing *ie* or *ei* letters to complete each word correctly.

55 ch_____f 56 f_____ld 57 w_____ght

58 bel_____ve 59 _____ght 60 rec_____ve

61 v_____n 62 th_____r

Copy the **proper nouns**, adding the missing capital letters.

63–69 duck prince edward wednesday

ship london football

everton football club lucy smith cargo

river severn gate parklands primary school

_____ _____

_____ _____

_____ _____

_____

Add a **verb** to these sentences. Each **verb** may be used only once.

Run Watch Pass Stop Find Hurry

70 _____ me a drink!

71 _____ out, you're standing on my toe!

72 _____ yourself a chair and sit down.

73 _____, he is going to catch you!

74 _____, a car is coming!

75 _____ up, we will be late!

Write two **antonyms** for each of these words.

76–77 big   _____   _____

78–79 rough   _____   _____

80–81 sensible   _____   _____

82–83 ugly   _____   _____

84–89 Instructional texts give us information on how best to do something.

Clearly write out the most effective way to play a playground game or make a recipe of your choice.

You will be marked on the organisation and layout of your instructions as well as how clear and useful they are.

_____

_____

_____

_____

_____

_____

Change the degree of possibility in these sentences by adding a different modal verb to each one, for example The children *should* sit in their seats.

90 The children _____ sit in their seats.

91 The children _____ sit in their seats.

92 The children _____ sit in their seats

93 The children _____ sit in their seats.

94 The children _____ sit in their seats..

6

D 9

8

C 7

6

D 6

5

Write a word to match each clue.

95 A musical instrument with strings   c_____

96 Long pieces of pasta   s_____

97 An animal from Australia that jumps   k_____

98 A hot drink, often drunk at breakfast   c_____

99 A red fruit, often served in salad   t_____

100 What do you notice about the last letter of each of the words above (Q. 96–99)?

_____   6

Now go to the Progress Chart to record your score!   **Total** 100

Paper 3

I dared not stir out of my castle for days, lest some savage should capture me. However, I gained a little courage and went with much dread to make sure that the footprint was not my own. I measured my foot against it. Mine was not nearly so large. A stranger, maybe a savage, must have been on shore, and fear again filled my heart.

I determined now to make my house more secure than ever. I built another wall   5
around it, in which I fixed six guns, so that, if need be, I could fire off six in two minutes. Then I planted young trees around. I feared my goats might be hurt or stolen from me, so I fenced round several plots of ground, as much out of sight as possible, and put some goats in each plot. All this while I lived with a terrible fear in my mind that I might one day meet an enemy. I had lived on this lonely island for eighteen years.   10

Once, when on the opposite side of the island, I was filled with horror; for on the ground I saw the remains of a fire, and also a number of human bones. This told me plainly that cannibals had been there.

From *Robinson Crusoe* by Daniel Defoe

Underline the correct answers.

1 How did Robinson Crusoe know the footprint was not his?
(it was a strange shape, it was larger than his, it was smaller than his)

2 How quickly could Robinson Crusoe fire his six guns?
(in 30 seconds, in one minute, in two minutes)

3 How long had Robinson Crusoe lived on the island?
(eighteen months, eight years, eighteen years)

3

Answer these questions.

4–5 Write the meaning of the words 'lest' (line 1) and 'plainly' (line 13) as they are used in this passage.

lest   _____

plainly   _____

6–7 How did Robinson Crusoe feel when he discovered cannibals were living on the island?

_____

Explain how you know this.

_____

8–10 Describe Robinson Crusoe's character in your own words.

Include lines or **phrases** from the text to support your answer.

_____

_____

_____

_____

_____

7

D 6

Underline the **nouns** in this passage.

11–21 My aunt, uncle and cousin came to stay with us last Wednesday. Next week we will catch a train to Birmingham. We are taking them to the theatre to see a pantomime called Aladdin. We will get back to our house very late.

11

Rewrite these sentences, adding the missing speech marks and other punctuation.

22–25 Come and hear the man play his banjo called Tim

_____

26–29 Where's my other slipper grumbled Grandpa

_____

Extend each of these words into a **compound word**.

30 tea_____   **31** sun_____

32 snow_____   **33** grand_____

34 pillow_____   **35** foot_____

36 tooth_____   **37** play_____

Write each of these words in its **plural** form.

38 brush _____   **39** church _____

40 child _____   **41** valley _____

42 thrush _____   **43** baby _____

Underline the **reported speech** sentences.

44–47 "Time to go Sam," called Mum.

Hank shouted to Ben to hurry up.

Kay moaned that Debbie was always late.

"Tuhil, are you coming?" shouted his teacher.

"Let's take the dog for a walk," pleaded the children.

The teacher told the children to leave by the fire exit.

"We had sausages for tea," said Maeve.

Mum told Gran that David's school report was good.

Rewrite these words adding the **suffix** _ing_ to each one.

48 drive _____   **49** believe _____

50 run _____   **51** care _____

52 close _____   **53** refer _____

54 transfer _____   **55** canoe _____

D 4
D 5
8
D 11
8
E 2
6
D 12
4
E 2
8

There is a lake near our town and it is very popular with both adults and children. The Sailing Club is at the south end of the lake and at the opposite end is a boathouse where visitors can hire various craft – sailing boats, rowing boats and canoes. Towards the middle of the lake on one side there is a part which is roped off. This is used for swimming. Sometimes a sailing boat capsizes, and as the water is not very deep this can provide much merriment for the onlookers! There are many reasons why a boat may capsize. Usually it is caused by a violent gust of wind, but it may be due to overloading, a faulty boat, or simply lack of skill in handling the craft.

Write *true* or *false* next to each statement.

56 The lake is only popular with children.   _____

57 The sailing club is at the north end of the lake.   _____

58 At the boathouse visitors can hire canoes.   _____

59 There is an area for swimming in the lake.   _____

60 The water in the lake is very deep.   _____

61 Overloading can cause boats to capsize.   _____

62 It is always the sailors' fault when a boat capsizes.   _____

7

C 4

Which creatures make these **onomatopoeic** noises?

63 Howl!   _____   64 Squawk!   _____

65 Snarl!   _____   66 Whinny!   _____

67 Coo   _____   68 Honk   _____

6

D 4

Add the missing commas to these sentences.

69 The wind swept over the barren landscape tossing leaves high into the air.

70 Although the speeding train came off its rails no one was hurt.

71 The lion crept up on its prey ready to pounce.

72–73 Reuben packed some snacks copying his sister to eat on the school trip.

74 Jess was delighted to see her mum though she wished she had come to collect her earlier.

6

E 2

Circle the words which have a soft *c*.

75–82 city   copy   cereal   face   magic   fleece

clown   mice   lace   accident   cabbage

vacuum   cat   jack   ace   carrot

8

With a line match the words with the same spelling patterns.

83 sound	match
84 high	hollow
85 fair	found
86 bridge	sigh
87 follow	fridge
88 hatch	chair

6

Rewrite each sentence as if you were writing about yourself.

Example: He enjoys running.   *I enjoy running.*

89 They fell over.   _____

90 She feels hot.   _____

91 He plays football.   _____

92 They walk home slowly.   _____

D 6

4

Add *ciuos* or *tious* to complete each word.

93 mali   _____   **94** infec   _____

95 ficti   _____   **96** deli   _____

97 suspi   _____   **98** cau   _____

99 pre   _____   **100** ambi   _____

D 6

8

Now go to the Progress Chart to record your score!   Total   100

A Servant for a Day by Kate Redman
23rd March

We arrived at Bourton House just after 10 o'clock. We were all
dressed in Victorian costume. I was wearing a plain brown dress
with black shoes and stockings. My hair was in a bun. I had a
shawl to keep me warm.   5

As soon as we arrived we were told off for being late. I thought
it wasn't our fault but was too scared to say anything.

Then we were given our instructions. We weren't allowed to
talk, had to walk everywhere quietly and if we were spoken to,   10
always had to say "Yes, ma'am" or "Yes, sir".

We were shown into the dining room where we were taught to
fold cotton napkins. It was very hard and Helen got told off for
making a mess of hers.

Then we went into the kitchens and were taught how to bake   15
bread. We all took it in turns to help, it was great fun and the
cook was really nice. She didn't mind if we talked and laughed.

Suddenly we heard a bell in the corridor. The bell told us we
were wanted in the bedrooms so we hurried up the stairs as quietly
as possible. Dan fell over! There we were told how to make the   20
bed and sweep the floor. When we swept the floor we had to put
damp tea leaves down; as we swept them up it helped to pick up
the dirt.

At last it was time to go back to school. We were told we had
been good servants and if we ever wanted a job we could have   25
one at Bourton House!

It was a great trip but I didn't like not being able to talk.

Underline the correct answers.

1 What period costume was Kate wearing?

(Viking, Victorian, Tudor)

2 Why did Kate wear a shawl?

(to look good, to hide her dress, to keep her warm)

3 Which room were they shown into first?

(the kitchen, the dining room, the bedroom)

4 Who got told off while folding a napkin?

(Helen, Kate, Dan)

4

Answer these questions.

5–6 Find two pieces of evidence from the text that suggest Victorian servants had to be quiet.

_____

_____

7–8 Which experience did Kate enjoy the most? Why?

_____

_____

9–11 Find three examples from the text that highlight the differences between Victorian times and now.

_____

_____

_____

7

Add the **prefix** pro or bi to each of these words.

E 2

12 _____lingual   13 _____claim   14 _____annual

15 _____noun   16 _____cycle   17 _____longed

6

Underline the correct form of the **verb** to complete each sentence.

D 6

18 The children watch/watches the match.

19 A cat play/plays with a mouse.

20 Winds sweep/sweeps across the land.

21 William run/runs to catch the bus.

18

22 The women win/wins the lottery.

23 Six children swim/swims for charity.

24 A leaf drop/drops from a tree.

7

Write one word for each **definition**.

25 Part of a plant that grows downwards and draws
food from the soil   _____

26 The time between dusk and dawn   _____

27 A grown-up person   _____

28 A member of the army   _____

29 A small white flower with a yellow centre   _____

30 A line of people, one behind another, waiting for their turn
to do something   _____

6

31–36 Write a short passage that includes at least two full stops, two question marks,
two exclamation marks and a pair of brackets.

D 5

_____

_____

_____

_____

_____

_____

6

B

> Squirrels are found in most countries. In Europe it is the red squirrel
> that is seen most, but in Britain the grey squirrel has been introduced
> from America. Flying squirrels do not really fly but glide from one tree
> to another. Ground squirrels may dig large numbers of burrows.

Underline the statements that are *true* and circle the statements that are *false*.

37–43 There are only grey squirrels in Britain.

Flying squirrels glide.

Grey squirrels first came from America.

Squirrels are found in Europe and elsewhere.

There are not many squirrels now.

A ground squirrel's home is called a tunnel.

Flying squirrels live in America only.

Add a different **adjective** in each gap to complete the sentences.

44 The Browns had a _____ clock in the hall.

45 They made a _____ crown for the king.

46 The _____ lady presented the prizes.

47 They went up the _____ staircase.

48 The _____ book looked as though it had been read many times.

49 The _____ kitten romped around the house.

Write the word for the young of each of these animals.

50 dog _____   51 pig _____

52 cat _____   53 horse _____

54 cow _____   55 goat _____

56 duck _____   57 sheep _____

Rewrite these sentences without the double negatives.

58 I'm not never coming back.

_____

59 Mark hasn't brought no towel for swimming.

_____

60 The shopkeeper didn't have no fireworks.

_____

61 There wasn't no teacher to help with my spelling.

_____

62 Amy hasn't no coat to wear.

_____

63 There weren't no goats on the farm.

_____

Complete these word sums.

64 attend + ant = _____   65 attend + ance = _____

66 assist + ant = _____   67 assist + ance = _____

68 confide + ent = _____   69 confide + ence = _____

70 correspond + ent = _____   71 correspond + ence = _____

E 2
8

Add one of the **prefixes** to each word to make its **antonym**.

un   in   im

72 _____expensive   73 _____possible

74 _____kind   75 _____mature

76 _____perfect   77 _____done

E 2
D 9
6

Write whether these sentences are written in the **past**, **present** or **future** tense.

78 I am eating.   _____

79 I will swim.   _____

80 I am reading.   _____

81 I ran home.   _____

82 I will brush my teeth.   _____

83 I have done my homework.   _____

D 6
6

Underline the **connectives** in each sentence.

84 The river broke its bank and many houses were flooded.

85 Dan cut himself, however, he didn't need a plaster.

86 Rani felt unwell, nevertheless she still went to school.

87 Harry agreed to go to the playground though he really wanted to go straight home.

88 Kim was given a prize but Henry has never won one.

89 The children weren't tired although it was past their bedtime.

D 2
6

Write the **antonym** for each of these words.

90 near _____   91 over _____

92 top _____   93 in _____

94 day _____   95 hot _____

6

Circle the words which have a soft *g*.

E 2

96–100 gate   giraffe   vegetable   game

gem   page   magic   goblin   wagon

5

Now go to the Progress Chart to record your score!   Total 100

Paper 5

Camouflage

B

Many animals are camouflaged by being of similar colour to the places where they
live. The polar bear who lives in the snowy far north has white fur. The kangaroo,
who lives in dry, dusty grassland, has sandy-coloured fur. The colour of the lion
blends in with the colour of dry grass found in hot countries. The tapirs, who live in
the jungles, have a colour pattern which seems of little use – the front of their   5
bodies, their heads and their legs are black, while the rest is white. We can pick out
tapirs easily at the zoo but in their homeland it is not so. They hunt at night when
there are patches of moonlight and patches of shadow and this is how they are
protected. Some animals, like the Arctic fox, who live in cold countries change the
colour of their coats in winter so that the new white coat will tone in with the snow.   10
Other animals have a dazzle pattern. A zebra's black and white stripes don't blend
in with its surroundings, but zebras feed in the early morning and late evening when
they cannot be seen so well. Their outline is broken up against the tall grasses and
trees and they become almost invisible.

Underline the correct answers.

1 What colour is a polar bear's fur?

(white, brown, sandy)

2 What environment does a kangaroo live in?

(jungle, snowy far north, dry dusty grassland)

3–4 Which two animals are black and white?

(polar bear, tapir, lion, Arctic fox, zebra)

4

Answer these questions.

5 Which animal lives in a hot country and has a coat the colour of dry grass?

_____

6 Two of the animals mentioned in the text are black and white. What else do they both have in common?

_____

7–8 What is interesting about the camouflage of the Arctic fox? Include a line from the text to support your answer.

_____

_____

_____

9 Write a **definition** for the word 'camouflage'.

_____

10 Why don't farm animals and pets need to be camouflaged?

_____

6

E 2

Change each of these **plurals** into its **singular** form.

11 churches   _____   **12** classes   _____

13 buses   _____   **14** bushes   _____

15 boxes   _____   **16** waltzes   _____

17 atlases   _____

18 Write a rule to be remembered when adding 'es' to make words plural.

_____

_____

8

D 6

Underline the **pronouns** in the sentences.

19–20 Mine is smaller than yours.

21–22 I am glad they have bought a dog.

23–24 You need to buy him a present.

25–26 Have you taken mine?

27–28 We have put ours over there.

10

Rewrite these book titles, adding the missing capital letters.

29–31 jason saves the day

_____

32–34 the history of the vikings

_____

35–38 football skills made fun

_____

D 6

10

Write a **synonym** for each of the words in bold.

39 The sailors were told to **abandon** the ship.   _____

40 The airman received an award for his **heroic** deed.   _____

41 I have **sufficient** money to buy it.   _____

42 She **enquired** how long she would have to wait.   _____

43 The **entire** school went on the outing.   _____

44 The children **dispersed** in all directions.   _____

45 The athlete **encountered** many difficulties.   _____

D 9

7

Add the missing apostrophes to each sentence.

46 Wheres your basket?

47 Isnt it over there?

48 Youll do it soon.

49 We shant do that!

50 I wont open the door.

51 We shouldve let her play with us.

52 Well have to go next time.

D 5

7

Put these towns in **alphabetical order**.

Norwich   Northwich   Northampton

Nottingham   Norwood   Northallerton

53 (1) _____   **54** (2) _____

55 (3) _____   **56** (4) _____

57 (5) _____   **58** (6) _____

E 2

6

Write five sentences, each with a relative clause beginning with the following words.

59 who _____

_____

60 that _____

_____

61 whom _____

_____

62 which _____

_____

63 whose _____

_____

5

E 2

Add the **suffix** to each of these words.

64 laugh + able   _____   **65** response + ible   _____

66 reason + able   _____   **67** combust + ible   _____

68 access + ible   _____   **69** adore + able   _____

70 consider + able   _____   **71** sense + ible   _____

8

D 6

Circle the **preposition** in each of these sentences.

72 The river flowed down the valley.

73 Karen hid behind the sofa.

74 Ethan and Meena struggled through the snow.

75 The zoo was behind the railway station.

76 Mum slept in the deckchair.

77 The cat jumped on the mouse.

78 The queen gracefully walked down the stairs.

79 The fish darted among the weeds.

8

Write *true* or *false* next to each of these statements.

80 The boy or girl must have a bicycle. _____

81 He/She would be needed six days a week. _____

82 Mr Jones wants a newsboy or girl quickly. _____

83 He/She would work nine hours a week. _____

84 Mr Jones doesn't mind if he employs a boy or a girl. _____

85 The pay would be £24 a week. _____

⬤ 6

Write a word with the same letter string but a different pronunciation underlined in each of these words.

86 h<u>ea</u>r _____ 87 e<u>igh</u>t _____ 88 thr<u>ough</u> _____

89 br<u>ave</u> _____ 90 <u>gi</u>ve _____ 91 n<u>ow</u> _____

⬤ 6

Add a powerful **verb** in the gaps to make each sentence interesting.

92 The children _____ over the bracken in their haste to get away.

93–94 Laila _____ at the top of her voice, making all the children

_____.

95 The cow _____ towards the milking parlour.

96 Sam _____ while watching the horror movie.

⬤ 5

Write four words that have entered our language in the last hundred years.

97–100 _____ _____ _____ _____

⬤ 4

Now go to the Progress Chart to record your score!   Total ⬤ 100

26

The Night Mail

This is the Night Mail crossing the Border,
Bringing the cheque and the postal order,

Letters for the rich, letters for the poor,
The shop at the corner, the girl next door.

Pulling up Beattock, a steady climb: 5
The gradient's against her, but she's on time.
Past cotton-grass and moorland boulder,
Shovelling white steam over her shoulder,

Snorting noisily, she passes
Silent miles of wind-bent grasses.   10

Birds turn their heads as she approaches,
Stare from bushes at her blank-faced coaches.

Sheep-dogs cannot turn her course;
They slumber on with paws across.

In the farm she passes no one wakes,   15
But a jug in a bedroom gently shakes.

Dawn freshens. Her climb is done.
Down towards Glasgow she descends,
Towards the steam tugs yelping down a glade of cranes,
Towards the fields of apparatus, the furnaces   20
Set on the dark plain like gigantic chessmen.
All Scotland waits for her:
In dark glens, beside pale-green lochs,
Men long for news.

by W H Auden

Underline the correct answers.

1 Beattock is a (station, hill, shop).

2 Birds turn their heads (to see what is making the noise, because they like watching trains, because they have stiff necks).

3 'Blank-faced coaches' are (ones with no lights, ones painted black, ones with no curtains).

Answer these questions.

4–6 What three items are we told the train is carrying?

_____

7 Why do you think W H Auden describes the steam as 'over her shoulder'(line 8)?

_____

8 Give the meaning of the word 'descends' (line 18), as it is used in the poem.

_____

9 What image does the line 'Set on the dark plain like gigantic chessmen' (line 21) bring to mind?

_____

_____

10 Which line in the poem is evidence that there is a farm close to the railway track?

_____

_____

7

E 2

Underline the **root word** of each of these words.

11 pressure	**12** detective	**13** blacken
14 recovered	**15** signature	**16** freshly
17 swimming	**18** unhelpful	

8

D 6

Circle the word which is:

19 a **pronoun**	children	came	we	go
20 a **verb**	football	goal	play	boys
21 an **adjective**	dog	friend	him	sad
22 an **adverb**	speed	I	come	quickly
23 a **noun**	he	aunt	strong	enrage
24 a **pronoun**	there	though	through	it
25 a **verb**	teach	children	camera	dinner

7

Underline the correct **homophone**.

26 The (lessen, lesson) started at eleven o'clock.

27 The man gave a (groan, grown) as he lifted the weight.

28 Dad said we must get a new ironing (board, bored).

29 The (lone, loan) sailor had crossed the ocean.

30 The gardener put in (steaks, stakes) for the sweet peas to climb.

31 Kang had (two, to) help his teacher.

32 Alice had an (hour, our) to wait.

7

Which type of noun (**common**, **proper**, **abstract** or **collective**) is each of these words?

33 Anna _____

34 crowd _____

35 fence _____

36 love _____

37 flock _____

38 Brazil _____

39 sympathy _____

7

With a line match each expression with its meaning.

40 to be hard up

41 to get into hot water

42 to have forty winks

43 to go on all fours

44 to play with fire

45 to face the music

46 to lead a dog's life

to be treated badly

to take punishment without complaint

to get into trouble

to ask for trouble

to be short of money

to crawl on hands and knees

to have a short sleep

7

Complete each sentence by adding a **conjunction**.

47 She didn't see me _____ I waved at her.

48 I have learned to swim _____ I have been at this school.

49 I cannot reach my books _____ you have moved that parcel.

50 David likes his tea very hot _____ Brygid doesn't like tea at all.

51 I couldn't sing _____ I had a sore throat.

52 Kerry has cut her finger _____ she will have to wash it.

53 I am very keen on swimming _____ I like diving too.

7

Rewrite these words adding the **suffix** *ery* or *ary*. Make any spelling changes necessary.

E 2

54 burgle _____

55 confection _____

56 jewel _____

57 moment _____

58 slip _____

59 diction _____

60 shrub _____

61 bound _____

8

Finish each sentence by adding a helper **verb** to match the **tense** in bold.

D 6

62 The car _____ speeding down the valley.   **past**

63 The birds _____ flying high in the sky.   **present**

64 A chicken _____ pecking in the dirt.   **present**

65 Two speed-boats _____ racing out to sea.   **past**

66 The sheep _____ flocking together on the moor.   **present**

67 A frog _____ jumping about in our pond.   **past**

6

Rewrite these sentences, adding the missing punctuation.

D 5

68–71 Can I have some of your drink asked Karen

_____

72–78 Are you up yet Jake's mum called It is time for school

_____

11

Write the short form we often use for each of these words.

D 8

79 telephone _____

80 bicycle _____

81 examination _____

82 photograph _____

83 hippopotamus _____

84 mathematics _____

6

Barncroft Primary School, Portsmouth, is putting on a play, *Nelson's Adventures*, portraying the adventures of Nelson in his flagship, the *Victory*. The whole school has worked on this drama project for the last week after visiting the ship. Richard Edmunds, who plays Nelson, is reported to have said that it has been the best week at school he has ever had.

The children are performing to the general public on Friday 4th and Saturday 5th November at 7.30 p.m. Mrs Danielle Turnpike, the headteacher, would like to encourage people from the local area to come and watch as they might learn something new about the historic ship moored at their city. All the money the performances earn will be given to 'Children in Need'.

Read the newspaper article and answer the questions.

85 Barncroft Primary School is putting on a play. What is it about?

_____

86 Who is playing Nelson?

_____

87 On what days of the week are the performances?

_____

88 Why will the play be particularly interesting to the people of Portsmouth?

_____

89 This newspaper article is missing a heading. Write your own heading for this article.

_____

Write a hypenated word using each prefix.

90 co _____

91 re _____

92 bi _____

93 cross _____

94 de _____

95 ex _____

Rewrite these sentences in the **future tense**.

96 She took a photo.

_____

97 I woke up at 7 o'clock.

_____

98 I enjoyed that piece of cake.

_____

99 It is raining.

_____

100 We played on the swings.

_____   5

Now go to the Progress Chart to record your score!   Total   100

The hyena once had the luck to come upon a dead ass. There was enough meat for three whole days. He was busy enjoying his meal when suddenly he saw his children coming. He knew their healthy young teeth and growing appetites, and as he did not want to share the magnificent carcass with them, he said: "You see that village over there? If you're quick you'll find plenty of asses there, just like this one. Only run." 5

The hyena's children rushed towards the village, shouting the news at the top of their voices. As the tale travelled to all corners of the bush, starving animals crept out – jackals, civet-cats, tiger-cats – all the smaller wild animals ran towards the village where the feast of asses' meat was to be found.

The whole morning the hyena watched them go by, singly or in flocks, until in 10 the end he began to be worried.

Well, he said to himself, it looks as if it must be true. That village must be full of dead asses. And leaving the carcass he had had all to himself, he started off to join a band of other animals who were running towards the village.

The Hyena and the Dead Ass a West African tale retold by René Guillot

Underline the correct answers.

    1 Why was the hyena lucky to find a dead ass?

       (It would keep him warm at night,

       It would feed his family,

       It would give him food for three days)

    2 What did the hyena's children do on their way to the village?

       (crept along quietly, rushed along shouting, crept along shouting)

  3–4 Who joined the hyena's children at the village?

       (asses, only jackals, the hyena, smaller wild animals)

4

Answer these questions.

5 Why didn't the hyena want his children to eat with him?

_____

6 Were there plenty of dead asses at the village? Explain your answer.

_____

7 How do you think the tale of the dead asses travelled to the corners of the bush?

_____

8–9 Why do you think the hyena joined the other animals in running towards the village? Include a line from the text to support your answer.

_____

_____

_____

Add the **suffix** to each of these words. Make any spelling changes necessary.

10 base + ment _____   **11** happy + ness _____

12 argue + ment _____   **13** spite + ful _____

14 use + ful _____   **15** lonely + ness _____

Underline the **adjectival phrase** in each sentence.

16 The hollow-eyed, pale-faced mask frightened the children.

17 The huge, mottled brown horse bounded about the field.

18 Snow fell from the twisted, broken branch.

19 The cold and fresh water tasted lovely.

20 George put on his warm, cosy jumper.

21 The long, smooth snake hid under the rock for protection.

With a line match the country from where you think each word is borrowed.

22 pasta   Australia

23 boomerang   China

24 wok   Italy

25 restaurant   America

26 moose   India

27 pyjamas   France

34

Complete each sentence using a different **adverb**.

28 I whispered _____.

29 We shouted _____.

30 I coughed _____.

31 We slept _____.

32 I cried _____.

33 We chuckled _____.

34 I laughed _____.

35 We argued _____.

Add the missing commas to these sentences.

36 Mark suddenly jumped the dog having caught him unawares.

37–38 Time and time again as the boat was tossed by the waves the helicopter crew tried to save the fishermen.

39–40 The shop which earlier had been bustling with shoppers was now quiet.

41–42 Susie and Tariq already soaked from the pouring rain ran to find cover.

Complete the following **adjectives** of comparison.

Example: good   *better*   *best*

43–44 rich   _____   _____

45–46 bad   _____   _____

47–48 quiet   _____   _____

49–50 pretty   _____   _____

51–52 many   _____   _____

53–54 early   _____   _____

Give one word for each of these **definitions**.

55 Can be used when eating. It has three or four prongs set on the end of a handle.   _____

56 A period of two weeks.   _____

57 A door fitting which makes a noise to attract the attention of someone inside.   _____

58 To say something aloud from memory.   _____

59 A doll worked by pulling wires or strings in a toy theatre.   _____

60 The long, vertical part of a plant that supports the leaves and flowers.   _____

61 A raised platform on which plays are often performed. _____

62 Thin rope, line or cord used for tying up parcels. _____

8

E 2

Write each of these words in their **plural** form.

63 half _____

64 shelf _____

65 thief _____

66 leaf _____

67 knife _____

68 calf _____

6

Copy the passage, adding the missing capital letters and punctuation.

D 4
D 5

69–87 quick shouted nina the water will trap us in the cave if we don't hurry
I know screamed james trying to be heard above the thundering waves
as james ran his feet barely touched the ground

_____

_____

_____

_____

_____

19

Write a word to match each picture.

E 2

88

_____

89

_____

90

_____

91

_____

4

E 2

92 All the words in questions 88–91 originate from the same country.

Which country is it? _____

1

pick	choice, choose, gather
piece	bit, chip, part, splinter, slice
pile	heap, collection, stack
plain	ordinary, unattractive, simple
pull	drag, tow, strain
push	force, persuade, poke, press

93 Write a word that has a similar meaning to 'plain'. _____

94 Write a word that has a similar meaning to 'tow'. _____

95 Write a synonym for the word 'push'. _____

96 Next to which word in bold would you put
the word 'tug'? _____

Underline the correct word in brackets.

97–98 An ambulance (is, are) speeding to the accident as many people (is, are) hurt.

99 There (was, were) a party at Sonia's house.

100 Many children (was, were) enjoying the firework display.

Now go to the Progress Chart to record your score! **Total** 100

Paper 8

One morning the girl was very thoughtful, and answered at random, and did not seem
to Toad to be paying proper attention to his witty sayings and sparkling comments.

'Toad,' she said presently, 'just listen, please. I have an aunt who is a
washerwoman.'

'There, there,' said Toad graciously and affably, 'never mind; think no more about   5
it. *I* have several aunts who *ought* to be washerwomen.'

'Do be quiet a minute, Toad,' said the girl. 'You talk too much, that's your chief
fault, and I'm trying to think, and you hurt my head. As I said, I have an aunt who
is a washerwoman; she does washing for all the prisoners in this castle – we try to
keep any paying business of that sort in the family, you understand. She takes   10
out the washing on Monday morning, and brings it in on Friday evening. This is a
Thursday. Now, this is what occurs to me: you're very rich – at least you're always
telling me so – and she's very poor. A few pounds wouldn't make any difference to
you, and it would mean a lot to her. Now, I think if she were properly approached
– squared, I believe, is the word you animals use – you could come to some   15

37

arrangement by which she would let you have her dress and bonnet and so on, and you could escape from the castle as the official washerwoman. You're very alike in many respects – particularly about the figure.'

'We're *not*,' said the Toad in a huff. 'I have a very elegant figure – for what I am.'

'So has my aunt,' replied the girl, 'for what *she* is. But have it your own way. You   20 horrid, proud ungrateful animal, when I'm sorry for you, and trying to help you!'

'Yes, yes, that's all right; thank you very much indeed,' said the Toad hurriedly. 'But look here! you wouldn't surely have Mr. Toad, of Toad Hall, going about the country disguised as a washerwoman!'

'Then you can stop here as a Toad,' replied the girl with much spirit. 'I suppose   25 you want to go off in a coach-and-four!'

Honest Toad was always ready to admit himself in the wrong. 'You are a good, kind, clever girl,' he said, 'and I am indeed a proud and stupid toad. Introduce me to your worthy aunt, if you will be so kind, and I have no doubt that the excellent lady and I will be able to arrange terms satisfactory to both parties.'   30

Next evening the girl ushered her aunt into Toad's cell, bearing his week's washing pinned up in a towel. The old lady had been prepared beforehand for the interview, and the sight of certain gold sovereigns that Toad had thoughtfully placed on the table in full view practically completed the matter and left little further to discuss. In return for his cash, Toad received a cotton print gown, an apron, a   35 shawl, and a rusty black bonnet; the only stipulation the old lady made being that she should be gagged and bound and dumped down in a corner.

From *The Wind in the Willows* by Kenneth Grahame

Underline the correct answers.

1 Why does the girl say her head hurts?

(she knocks it, Toad talks too much, Toad upset her)

2 What day of the week is it at the beginning of this passage?

(Monday, Thursday, Friday)

   2

Answer these questions.

3–4 How does Toad feel about washerwomen in the beginning of the story? Pick out one piece of evidence to support your view.

_____

_____

5–6 Describe in your own words how you would have felt about Toad's reaction to the suggestion that he escapes the castle as a washerwoman, if you were the girl.

_____

_____

7 Why are some of the words in the passage written in *italics*?

_____

   5

8–10 The girl describes Toad as a 'horrid, proud and ungrateful animal' (line 21). Why do you think she used each of these **adjectives**?

_____

_____

_____

11–12 What was the washerwoman's only demand and why do you think she made it?

_____

_____

5

D 9

Write two **antonyms** for each word.

13–14 ugly _____ _____

15–16 right _____ _____

17–18 sad _____ _____

19–20 kind _____ _____

21–22 whisper _____ _____

10

D 6

Underline the correct word in the brackets.

23 Tim (done, did) his homework.

24 Every boy (were, was) on the field.

25 They (are, was) late today.

26 All the men (were, was) working.

27 I (have, shall) eaten all the cakes.

28 We (have, shall) take the dog for a walk.

29 I dropped the bag but not one of the eggs (has, shall) broken.

30 They (will, were) collect the old bed.

8

E 2

Change these words into verbs by adding _en_, _ise_ or _ify_.

31 drama _____ 32 solid _____

33 magnet _____ 34 thick _____

35 terror _____ 36 weak _____

37 black _____ 38 fertile _____

8

Next to each word write another word with the same *ough* sound.

39 bought _____ 40 thorough _____

41 rough _____ 42 plough _____

43 though _____.

Rewrite these sentences and add the missing punctuation.

44–47 When can we go swimming asked Jenny

_____

48–51 We will be late Mum yelled

_____

In each gap add a **connective**.

    although   where   because   which

52 The ship had called at many ports, finally arriving in Dublin _____ the sailors could go on leave.

53 Wendy was soaking _____ she had fallen in the river.

54 Daniel always found maths very difficult _____ he tried very hard.

55 Mum bought a new jumper _____ came with a free skirt.

Write *there, their* or *they're* in each of the gaps. Don't forget capital letters, if necessary.

56 I would like to go _____ today.

57 _____ waiting for the bus.

58 I like the colour of _____ school uniform.

59 "What a huge amount of work _____ is to do," sighed Mark.

60–61 The children were told to put _____ books inside _____ bags.

62 _____ very quiet!

63–64 They put _____ coats over _____.

Write the **abbreviations** of these words.

65 kilometre   _____

66 United Kingdom   _____

67 compact disc   _____

68 Member of Parliament _____

69 United States of America _____

70 television _____

71 Doctor _____

Add *anything* or *nothing* to each of these sentences.

72 David didn't say _____ as he travelled to school.

73 "There is _____ to do," moaned Tanya.

74 Nasar can't find _____ in his messy room.

75 Sonia didn't have _____ for breakfast.

76 There is _____ to paint with.

77 It is _____ to do with me!

Rewrite these sentences as **reported speech**.

78 "Where is my bag?" asked Ben.

_____

79 "We need to be quick," said Dad.

_____

80 "Can we go to the fair?" asked the children.

_____

81 "We are going to bake a cake," the teacher explained.

_____

Write a **synonym** for the word in bold.

82 The house was **vacant** for some time. _____

83 It was **suspended** from the ceiling. _____

84 The girl was very **conceited**. _____

85 Michael had **completed** his work. _____

86 He treated the horse **brutally**. _____

87 She **comprehended** what the man said. _____

Write whether each word is a **noun** or a **verb**.

Example: inform   *verb*

88 suggestion   _____

89 cloudiness   _____

90 conservation   _____

91 discuss   _____

92 insulate   _____

93 specialise   _____

NO DOGS IN OUR PLAYGROUND

Keep dogs away from our playground because ...

❏ they frighten some children

❏ they get in the way of the swings

❏ they leave a mess

Please walk your dogs in the park area around the duck pond.

Write *true*, *false* or *don't know* next to each statement.

94 Dogs are allowed in the playground.   _____

95 There is a slide in the playground.   _____

96 Dogs frighten all children.   _____

97 Dogs should be walked in the park area.   _____

98 Dogs can be in the playground if they are with their owners.   _____

99 Dogs never leave a mess.   _____

100 The park has a duck pond.   _____

D 6

6

B

7

Now go to the Progress Chart to record your score!   **Total**   100

Journey Home

I remember the long homeward ride, begun
By the light that slanted in from the level sun;
And on the far embankment, in sunny heat,
Our whole train's shadow travelling dark and complete.
A farmer snored. Two loud gentlemen spoke   5
Of the cricket and news. The pink baby awoke
And gurgled awhile. Till slowly out of the day
The last light sank in glimmer and ash-grey.
I remember it all; and dimly remember, too,
The place where we changed – the dark trains lumbering through;   10
The refreshment room, the crumbs, and the slopped tea;
And the salt on my face, not of tears, not tears, but the sea.
"Our train at last!" said Father. "Now tumble in!
It's the last lap home!" And I wondered what 'lap' could mean;
But the rest is all lost, for a huge drowsiness crept   15
Like a yawn upon me; I leant against Mother and slept.

by John Walsh

Underline the correct answers.

1 The weather was (cold, stormy, sunny, grey).

2–3 In the poem two people and the baby slept. Who were they?

(a gentleman, a farmer, me).

Answer these questions.

4 What words show that the baby might be happy?

_____

5 Where did the family wait for their second train?

_____

6 What do you think 'the last lap home' means? (line 14)

_____

7–8 Where have the family been? Copy a line from the poem to support your answer.

_____

_____

Now read the first verse of *From a Railway Carriage* by R L Stevenson.

Faster than fairies, faster than witches,
Bridges and houses, hedges and ditches;
And charging along like troops in a battle,
All through the meadows the horses and cattle;
All of the sights of the hill and the plain   5
Fly as thick as driving rain;
And ever again, in the wink of an eye,
Painted stations whistle by.

9–10 This poem was also written about a train journey. What do you notice about the pace of this poem? What is the pace trying to convey to the reader?

_____

_____   ◯ 2

In your own words describe what is meant by:

11–12 'All of the sights of the hill and the plain
Fly as thick as driving rain;' (lines 5–6)

_____

_____   ◯ 2

13–15 Find three different words that highlight the speed at which the train is moving.

_____ (line ____)

_____ (line ____)

_____ (line ____)   ◯ 3

Write each of these words in its **plural form**.   E 2

16 fly	_____	**17** bully	_____
18 valley	_____	**19** journey	_____
20 lady	_____	**21** hobby	_____
22 cry	_____	**23** donkey	_____	◯ 8

Write a suitable **preposition** in each gap.

D 6

on   with   behind   over   from   up

24 He ran _____ the stairs.

25 The teacher was cross _____ the cheeky boy.

26 Your t-shirt is different _____ mine.

27 The boy climbed _____ the wall.

28 The mouse hid _____ the bush.

29 Dad hid the present _____ the cupboard.

6

D 5

Rewrite these sentences, adding the missing apostrophes.

30 Rosies knitting was finished at last.

_____

31 Tonys dog ran away last week.

_____

32 The two boys football went over the fence.

_____

33 The three rabbits hutches fell down in the wind.

_____

34 Carolines leg hurt after she slipped on the ice.

_____

35 My mothers bedroom was a mess.

_____

6

E 2

Next to each word write another word with the same spelling pattern.

36 light   _____   37 love   _____

38 bridge   _____   39 bull   _____

40 boast   _____   41 core   _____

42 range   _____   43 ditch   _____

8

Complete the table below.

44–52

	er	est	ish
long			
small			
late			

9

With a line match the **dialect** words with their meaning.

53 nowt	eat
54 scoff	potatoes
55 wee	child
56 aye	yes
57 bairn	headache
58 tatties	nothing
59 skullache	little

7

Copy these sentences and add the missing punctuation and capital letters.

60–62 the candles blew out plunging the children into darkness

_____

63–65 carrying piles of apples the carts were pulled down the road

_____

66–68 high in the sky the birds were feeding on the flying insects

_____

9

Abbreviate these words into their **abbreviations** or **acronyms**.

69 United Nations   _____

70 British Broadcasting Corporation   _____

71 Royal Air Force   _____

72 North Atlantic Treaty Organisation _____

73 Justice of the Peace   _____

74 Heavy Goods Vehicle   _____

75 Criminal Investigation Department _____

7

Use words from the passage to complete the table.

> The small, weak rabbit searched frantically in the cave looking for food but all it could find behind a rock were the remains of a mouldy turnip. The rabbit sighed loudly and continued the search.

76–87

Noun	Adjective	Verb	Adverb	Preposition	Conjunction

Write four words with a silent letter.

88 _____

89 _____

90 _____

91 _____

Rewrite each sentence as though you are writing about someone else.

Example: I feel cold. *She feels cold.*

92 I stroke the dog. _____

93 I cry loudly. _____

94 I wash my hair. _____

95 I cook a meal. _____

Write the masculine form of each of these words.

96 duck _____

97 actress _____

98 princess _____

99 heroine _____

100 landlady _____

In the moonlight, Sophie caught a glimpse of an enormous long pale wrinkly face with the most enormous ears. The nose was as sharp as a knife, and above the nose there were two bright flashing eyes, and the eyes were staring straight at Sophie. There was a fierce and devilish look about them.

Sophie gave a yelp and pulled back from the window. She flew across the dormitory and jumped into her bed and hid under the blanket. 5

And there she crouched, still as a mouse, and tingling all over.

Under the blanket Sophie waited.

After a minute or so, she lifted a corner of the blanket and peeped out.

For the second time that night her blood froze to ice and she wanted to scream, but no sound came out. There at the window, with the curtains pushed aside, was the enormous long pale wrinkly face of the Giant Person, staring in. The flashing black eyes were fixed on Sophie's bed. 10

The next moment, a huge hand with pale fingers came snaking in through the window. This was followed by an arm, an arm as thick as a tree-trunk, and the arm, the hand, the fingers were reaching out across the room towards Sophie's bed. 15

This time Sophie really did scream, but only for a second because very quickly the huge hand clamped down over her blanket and the scream was smothered by the bedclothes.

Sophie, crouching underneath the blanket, felt strong fingers grasping hold of her, and then she was lifted up from her bed, blanket and all, and whisked out of the window. 20

If you can think of anything more terrifying than that happening to you in the middle of the night, then let's hear about it.

The awful thing was that Sophie knew exactly what was going on although she couldn't see it happening. She knew that a Monster (or Giant) with an enormous long pale wrinkly face and dangerous eyes had plucked her from her bed in the middle of the witching hour and was now carrying her out through the window smothered in a blanket. 25

What actually happened next was this. When the Giant had got Sophie outside, he arranged the blanket so that he could grasp all the four corners of it at once in one of his huge hands, with Sophie imprisoned inside. In the other hand he seized the suitcase and the long trumpet thing and off he ran. 30

From *The BFG* by Roald Dahl

Underline the correct answers.

1 At what time of day does the passage take place?

(day-time, night-time, can't tell)

2 How was the Giant Person's nose described?

(as long as a knife, as pointed as a knife, as sharp as a knife)

3 Where did Sophie run to?

(the other side of the room, into her bed, behind the curtain)

○ 3

Answer these questions.

4–5 Give the meaning of the following words as they are used in the passage.

'devilish' (line 4) _____

'crouched' (line 7) _____

6 Why do you think no sound came out when Sophie wanted to scream (line 11)?

_____

7–8 Write two **adjectives** found in the passage that describe the Giant's face.

_____ (line ____)

_____ (line ____)

9–10 Copy the line from the passage where the author communicates directly with the reader. Why do you think he does this?

_____

_____

_____

11–12 Describe the Giant in your own words, using evidence in the passage.

_____

_____

13–15 Describe the way Sophie is feeling as she is carried in the blanket. Include a line or phrase from the passage to support your answer.

_____

_____

_____

○ 12

49

Add the **suffix** to each of these words. Don't forget any spelling changes.

16 shy + ly _____

17 spy + ed _____

18 try + ed _____

19 easy + er _____

20 dry + ing _____

21 cry + ed _____

Copy the passage, adding the missing capital letters.

22–31 suddenly, out of the tunnel emerged the flying scotsman. hannah and leroy had been waiting for this moment, ever since reading about this train in famous trains of the past. they screamed with excitement as it flew past them on its way to banbury.

_____

_____

_____

_____

_____

Write two **compound words** that begin with the word in bold.

32–33 every _____   _____

34–35 candle _____   _____

36–37 rain _____   _____

38–39 play _____   _____

Write each of these **adverbs** in a sentence.

40 angrily

_____

41 stupidly

_____

42 unexpectedly

_____

Complete the table of **nouns** below.

43–54 France   love   team   door   sympathy   leg   Nigel

      camel   justice   bunch   swarm   Hyde Park

Common nouns	Proper nouns	Collective nouns	Abstract nouns

Add *cial* or *tial* to complete the words.

55 offi_____   **56** confiden_____

57 essen_____   **58** commer_____

59 artifi_____   **60** par_____

Add an **adjectival phrase** to complete each sentence.

61 Tola slept peacefully in her _____ bed.

62 The _____ fireworks went high in the sky.

63 Alice clutched her _____ teddy.

64 Monty, the _____ dog, bounded through the long grass.

Add a **prefix** to each of these **words** to make a new word.

65 activate _____   **66** join _____

67 treat _____   **68** embark _____

69 continue _____   **70** define _____

71 compose _____   **72** head _____

Put a *tick* next to the words spelt correctly and a *cross* next to those spelt incorrectly.

73 shreik _____

74 rein _____

75 leisure _____

76 releive _____

77 niegh _____

78 receive _____

79 seige _____

7

Underline the two **clauses** in each sentence.

D 2

80–81 Aden ran with all his might when he saw the raging bull.

82–83 Julie combed her hair constantly because she wanted straight hair.

84–85 While Yan was painting a picture, the lights suddenly went off.

6

Write a sentence using brackets to indicate parenthesis.

D 5

86–87 _____

_____

Write a sentence using dashes to indicate parenthesis.

88–89 _____

_____

Write a sentence using commas to indicate parenthesis.

90–91 _____

_____

6

Write down three **onomatopoeic** words that can be used with these.

C 4

92–94 fireworks

_____   _____   _____

95–97 rain

_____   _____   _____

98–100 a farmyard

_____   _____   _____

9

Paper 11

What is a hobbit? I suppose hobbits need some description nowadays since they
have become rare and shy to the Big People, as they call us. They are (or were)
a little people, about half our height, and smaller than the bearded Dwarves.
Hobbits have no beards. There is little or no magic about them, except the ordinary
everyday sort which helps them to disappear quietly and quickly when large stupid   5
folk like you and me come blundering along, making a noise like elephants which
they can hear a mile off. They are inclined to be fat in the stomach; they dress in
bright colours (chiefly green and yellow); wear no shoes because their feet grow
natural leather soles and thick warm brown hair like the stuff on their heads (which
is curly); have long brown fingers, good natured faces and laugh deep fruity laughs   10
especially after dinner which they have twice a day when they can get it).

From *The Hobbit* by J R R Tolkien

Underline the correct answers.

1 What magic can hobbits do?

(make themselves smaller, disappear quickly and quietly, make magic shoes)

2 What creatures do hobbits think make a lot of noise?

(elephants, dwarves, people)

3 What colour is a hobbit's skin?

(white, black, pink, brown)

Answer these questions.

4 Why might good hearing be an advantage to hobbits?

_____

5–6 Write two reasons why hobbits don't need to wear shoes.

_____

_____

7 Copy the **phrase** from the text that suggests hobbits might enjoy their food.

_____

_____

8 Describe in the context of the passage what 'good natured faces' (line 9–10) means.

_____

9–11 Find three examples where the writer highlights the differences between the 'Big People' and hobbits.

_____

_____

_____

12–14 Imagine you are a hobbit. Write a short passage describing what you feel about the 'Big People'. Use information from the text to support your answer.

_____

_____

_____

_____

○ 11

E 2

Circle only the words that _are not_ **homophones**.

15–23 diner   dinner   vain   vein   vane   bath   bathe

cite   site   sight   sit   through   threw   thorough

rain   reign   rein   passed   past   pasted

grisly   grizzly   lung   lunge   missed   mist

○ 9

E 2

Change these words into their **singular** form.

24 skies   _____   **25** lives   _____

26 lorries   _____   **27** giraffes   _____

28 oxen   _____   **29** posies   _____

○ 6

D 5

Write three sentences, each sentence must include two **possessive pronouns**.
Underline each **possessive pronoun**.

30–31 _____

32–33 _____

34–35 _____

○ 6

54

Add a **conjunction** to complete each sentence.

36 The rain poured in through the window _____ no one noticed.

37 I knew where my toothbrush should be _____ I couldn't find it.

38 The dog scratched at the door _____ someone let him in.

39 I like fish and chips _____ I am feeling hungry.

40 Sheena loves reading _____ also writing stories.

41 Deano was tired _____ he didn't want to go to bed.

6

E 2

Choose the correct **prefix** to complete each word.

| bi | circum | auto | tele |

42 _____phone

43 _____motive

44 _____navigate

45 _____plane

46 _____vision

47 _____biography

48 _____scope

49 _____focals

8

Complete the table below.

strange	coffee	really	jumped	into	of
curly	with	truly	it	himself	threw
almost	thin	going	you	horror	scoundrel

50–67

Nouns	Verbs	Adjectives	Adverbs	Prepositions	Pronouns

18

Add *was* or *were* in each gap to complete each sentence.

68–69 They _____ ready to go swimming but the pool _____ not open.

70 All the children had finished their lunch and _____ ready to go out to play.

71–72 They _____ queuing for hours as the film _____ supposed to be brilliant.

73 Sam wondered whether it _____ time to get up.

Choose a word to complete each expression.

blanket   fence   head   rat   seat   leaf   horse

74 to hang your _____

75 to be a wet _____

76 to turn over a new _____

77 to take a back _____

78 to put the cart before the _____

79 to smell a _____

80 to sit on the _____

Use each of these **prepositions** in an amusing sentence.

81 against

_____

82 between

_____

83 through

_____

84 below

_____

Complete the table below by matching each word to its country of origin. For example the word café originated from France.

café   gondola   boutique   macaroni   tortilla

mosquito   opera   armadillo   adieu

France	Spain	Italy
café		

8

D 5

Write a **contraction** for each of these pairs of words.

93 we shall _____

94 they will _____

95 should not _____

96 I have _____

97 has not _____

98 will not _____

99 there is _____

100 you are _____

8

Now go to the Progress Chart to record your score!   Total **100**

There is an old legend about Delhi (the capital of India). Long ago an old Hindu king was hammering a large iron nail into the earth, and as he swung with all his might the tip of the nail struck the head of the snake-god who supports the world on his coiled body. The king trembled at the thought of the snake-god's anger – would he bring fire and plague to his subjects, or even destroy the world? He ordered all his   5
subjects to offer prayers and sacrifices to placate the snake-god. Several months passed and when the god's anger was soothed he told the king that he wouldn't punish him, but he said that on that spot there would always be war and unrest.

The iron nail in this fable is supposed to be the Iron Pillar which today stands in the courtyard of a tower built about six hundred years ago. There is another legend which   10
says that if you stand with your back to the pillar and can stretch your arms behind you around the pillar, all your wishes will come true. Many people have tried to do this but no one has had arms long enough to get more than half way round the pillar!

Underline the correct answers.

1 In which country is the city of Delhi?

(India, Iran, Indonesia)

2 What are the king's 'subjects'?

(words, people, thoughts, towns)

3 How long ago was the tower that houses the Iron Pillar built?

(sixty years ago, six thousand years ago, six hundred years ago)

Answer these questions.

4 In the context of this passage, what does the **phrase** 'with all his might' (line 2) mean?

_____

5–6 What evidence is there that the king was concerned for his kingdom? Include a line or **phrase** from the passage to support your answer.

_____

_____

7 Write another word or **phrase** for 'sacrifices' (line 6).

_____

8–9 In your own words describe how you as the Hindu king might have felt the moment the nail struck the head of the snake-god. Explain why you would feel this way.

_____

_____

10–11 If you were the Hindu king and one day all your wishes were granted, what would you wish for?

_____

8

E 2

Add the **prefix** in or im to each of these words.

12 _____perfect   **13** _____correct   **14** _____accurate

15 _____pure   **16** _____balance   **17** _____complete

18 _____patient   **19** _____visible

8

D 12

Rewrite these direct speech sentences into **reported speech**.

20 "Time for dinner," called Mum.

_____

21 "Can we go out to play?" asked the children.

_____

22 "I'm hiding in the shed," David whispered to Amie.

_____

23 "It is really cold today," mumbled the postman.

_____

24 "I love my new shoes," exclaimed Gina.

5

_____

Write an **onomatopoeic** word for each of the following.

25 a bag of crisps _____

26 out of breath _____

27 tramping through mud _____

28 a bouncing ball _____

29 closing a door _____

30 diving in water _____

31 a watch alarm _____

7

Add the **suffix** *ed* to each of these words. Make any necessary spelling changes.

32 fit _____ 33 carry _____

34 knot _____ 35 pick _____

36 marry _____ 37 hunt _____

6

Write each of these pairs of short sentences as one sentence.

38 Tom ate his food. He was very hungry.

_____

39 The sun shone brightly. It woke Gemma up.

_____

40 The school trip was great fun. They didn't want to go home.

_____

41 Nasar learnt his spelling homework. He still got some wrong in the test.

_____

_____

4

Write whether each of these sentences is in the **past**, **present** or **future tense**.

42 The dog licked Grant. _____

43 Caitlin was swimming. _____

44 Len is sleeping. _____

45 The chicken is laying an egg. _____

46 I shall not be home till six o'clock. _____

47 Cleo ate her food. _____

48 Rachel will go to Matthew's house. _____ ⃝ 7

D 6

Write the words in the correct columns of the table.

49–60 stumbled　　frantically　　because　　of　　silky　　among

　　　　heaved　　beauty　　stupidly　　fluffy　　bread　　although

Noun	Adjective	Verb	Adverb	Preposition	Conjunction

⃝ 12

D 9

Write a **synonym** for each word in bold.

61 I **attempted** to climb the rock. _____

62 She was **requested** to sit down and wait. _____

63 He **remarked** that he was cold and tired. _____

64 The picture **adhered** to the paper. _____

65 She **frequently** went to see her grandmother. _____

66 Jack was **awarded** the first prize. _____

67 Shaun's family was very **wealthy**. _____

68 At the concert we **applauded** loudly. _____ ⃝ 8

E 2
D 6

Remove the **suffix** of these **abstract nouns** to make a **verb**.

69 attraction _____

70 entertainment _____

71 departure _____

72 attachment _____

73 failure _____

74 completion _____ ⃝ 6

Fill in the missing words in this poem.

> A stranger called this morning
> Dressed all in black and grey
> Put every sound into a bag

75 And carried them _____

> The whistling of the kettle
> The turning of the lock
> The purring of the kitten

76 The ticking of the _____

> The popping of the toaster
> The crunching of the flakes
> When you spread the marmalade

77 The scraping noise it _____

> The hissing of the frying-pan
> The ticking of the grill
> The bubbling of the bathtub

78 As it starts to _____

> The drumming of the raindrops
> On the window-pane
> When you do the washing-up

79 The gurgle of the _____

> The crying of the baby
> The squeaking of the chair
> The swishing of the curtain

80 The creaking of the _____

> A stranger called this morning
> He didn't leave his name
> Left us only silence

81 Life will never be the _____

'The Sound Collector' by Roger McGough

Rewrite these sentences without double negatives.

82 I haven't got no money.

_____

83 There wasn't no clown at the circus.

_____

84 There weren't no sweets in the jar.

_____

85 Tina hasn't no umbrella for the rain.

_____ 4

D 4

D 5

Rewrite the following correctly.

86–100 quick come here called tom
the rain was falling heavily and they wanted to avoid getting wet
when do you think it will stop asked misha

_____

_____

_____

_____ 15

Progress Chart   English 9–10 years Book 1

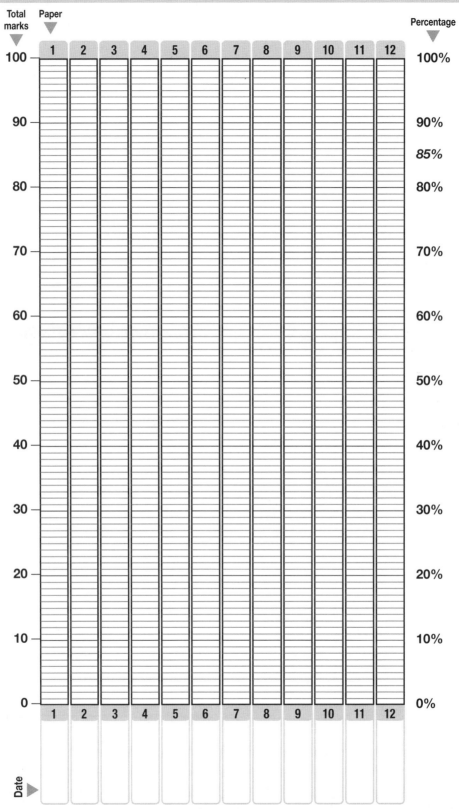

Total marks

Paper

Percentage

| 1 | 2 | 3 | 4 | 5 | 6 | 7 | 8 | 9 | 10 | 11 | 12 |

100 — 100%

90 — 90%

85%

80 — 80%

70 — 70%

60 — 60%

50 — 50%

40 — 40%

30 — 30%

20 — 20%

10 — 10%

0 — 0%

| 1 | 2 | 3 | 4 | 5 | 6 | 7 | 8 | 9 | 10 | 11 | 12 |

Date ▶

When you've finished the book use the Next Step Planner ➤

Some questions will be answered in the children's own words. Answers to these questions are given in *italics*. Any answers that seem to be in line with these should be marked correct.

Paper 1

1 butter
2 gas
3 sugar and ginger
4 *stodgy, lacking in air, hard*
5–6 Description on using the oven e.g. 'Now you had better light your oven gas' and 'If you are cooking by a kitchen range...'. The ingredients are measured in ounces.
7–10 *Wash the currants in tepid water twice.*
Rub them with a cloth.
Put them in a warm oven to dry but not cook.
Once dry check all the currants have their stalks removed.
11–12 scent, sent
13–14 threw, through
15–16 knot, not
17–18 pane, pain
19–20 stare, stairs
21 ⓟ
22 ⓦ
23 ⓓ
24 ⓣ
25 ⓑ
26 ⓝ
27–29 Sam loved going for walks, swimming in the duck pond, chasing rabbits, chewing a bone and sleeping in front of the fire.
30–31 The baby cries when it is tired, hungry, has a tummy ache or has a dirty nappy.
32–34 Jack wanted a new bike, some colouring pens, a computer game, new trainers and a pet dog for his birthday!
35–41 gatepost, York, Monday, bunch, banana, violin, team
42 neatly
43 greedily
44 heavily
45 soundly
46 swiftly
47 suddenly
48 smartly
49 telephones
50 thieves
51 museums
52 churches
53 tragedies
54 roofs
55 !
56 .
57 ! or .
58 ?
59 ?
60 .
61 !
62–64 The girl ran to catch her bus.
65–66 He/She had collected money to give to the homeless child.
67–69 The lamb bounced towards its mother.
70–75 <u>We</u> are going to Hull to see the docks.
<u>We</u> will see several ships and if <u>we</u> are lucky <u>they</u> might let <u>us</u> look around <u>them</u>.
76 destroy
77 nasty
78 happy
79 willing
80 delighted
81 tiny
82 Give yourself a hug
83–84 any two of: *When you feel unloved, when people put on airs, when people give a cold-shoulder shrug.*
85 *When people ignore you.*
86–87 *The final verse emphasises how special each and every one of us is.*
'Only one in a million-billion-trillion-zillion like me.'

88 careful
89 dutiful
90 plentiful
91 beautiful
92 wonderful
93–94 the three dogs' collars
95–96 the two cinemas' screens
97–98 the three boys' books
99–100 the two houses' chimneys

Paper 2

1 Monday
2 Thursday
3 Monday
4–5 'Tuesday's gales bashed elm and ash; dead branches came down with a crash'
6–8 arm, land, today
9–10 The first two lines rewritten as if it is a summer's day. The two lines need to rhyme and have a similar structure to the original poem, e.g. *On Monday the sun was out all day, so all the children went out to play.*
11–17 Seven of the following verbs: poured, flooded, bashed, came, walked, stood, was, bit, freeze, smashed, fell
18 **The goats pushed their way out of their pen** because they had spotted some apples.
19 **The cars raced past us** while we waited at the side of the motorway.
20 **Matthew's present was quickly hidden under the sofa** as he came in through the door.
21 **Some children wanted to go swimming** even though the water was freezing.
22 **The hat fitted perfectly** but it was the wrong colour.
23 **It started to rain heavily** as darkness fell over the sleepy village.
24 un<u>happy</u>
25 <u>jumped</u>
26 <u>quickly</u>
27 dis<u>place</u>ment
28 un<u>certain</u>
29 af<u>fix</u>
30 un<u>tie</u>
31 <u>stronger</u>
32 mis<u>trusted</u>
33 cough
34 height
35 foot
36 have
37 both
38 move
39 flower
40 drought
41–42 Yours looks longer than mine.
43–44 Ours is smaller than his.
45–46 Theirs runs faster than ours.
47 waiter
48 uncle
49 king
50 nephew
51 man
52 bull
53 fox
54 duke
55 chief
56 field
57 weight
58 believe
59 eight
60 receive
61 vein
62 their
63–69 Prince Edward, Wednesday, London, Everton Football Club, Lucy Smith, River Severn, Parklands Primary School
70 Pass
71 Watch
72 Find
73 Run
74 Stop
75 Hurry

76–77 *small, tiny*
78–79 *smooth, slippery*
80–81 *silly, foolish*
82–83 *pretty, beautiful*
84–89 The child's instructions on how to play a playground game or make a recipe. Marks for organisation and layout of information plus how clear and useful the instructions are.
90–94 *will, might, must, can, may, shall*
95 cello
96 spaghetti
97 kangaroo
98 coffee or cocoa
99 tomato
100 *The last letter of each word is a vowel.*

Paper 3

1 It was larger than his
2 in two minutes
3 eighteen years
4–5 *lest – in case*
   plainly – clearly
6–7 *horrified, scared.*
   He says that when he saw the human bones he was filled with horror.
8–10 The child's description of the type of person Robinson Crusoe was with evidence drawn from the passage, e.g. *Robinson Crusoe is clever because he has been able to survive on an island by himself for eighteen years.*
11–21 My <u>aunt</u>, <u>uncle</u> and <u>cousin</u> came to stay with us last <u>Wednesday</u>. Next <u>week</u> we will catch a <u>train</u> to <u>Birmingham</u>. We are taking them to the <u>theatre</u> to see a <u>pantomime</u> called <u>Aladdin</u>. We will get back to our <u>house</u> very late.
22–25 "Come and hear the man play his banjo," called Tim.
26–29 "Where's my other slipper?" grumbled Grandpa.
30 *teacup, teaspoon*
31 *sunshine, sunglasses*
32 *snowball, snowflake*
33 *grandfather, grandmother*
34 *pillowcase*
35 *football, footfall*
36 *toothache, toothbrush*
37 *playtime, playground*
38 brushes   39 churches
40 children   41 valleys
42 thrushes   43 babies
44–47 <u>Hank shouted to Ben to hurry up.</u>
   <u>Kay moaned that Debbie was always late.</u>
   <u>The teacher told the children to leave by the fire exit.</u>
   <u>Mum told Gran that David's school report was good.</u>
48 driving   49 believing
50 running   51 caring
52 closing   53 referring
54 transferring 55 canoeing
56 false   57 false
58 true   59 true
60 false   61 true
62 false

63 *dog, wolf*   64 *parrot, chicken*
65 *lion, dog*   66 *horse*
67 *dove, pigeon*   68 *goose*
69 The wind swept over the barren landscape, tossing leaves high into the air.
70 Although the speeding train came off its rails, no one was hurt.
71 The lion crept up on its prey, ready to pounce.
72–73 Reuben packed some snacks, copying his sister, to eat on the school trip.
74 Jess was delighted to see her mum, though she wished she had come to collect her earlier.
75–82 city, cereal, face, fleece, mice, lace, accident, ace
83 sound – found
84 high – sigh
85 fair – chair
86 bridge – fridge
87 follow – hollow
88 hatch – match
89 I fell over.
90 I feel hot.
91 I play football.
92 I walk home slowly.
93 malicious
94 infectious
95 fictitious
96 delicious
97 suspicious
98 cautious
99 precious
100 ambitious

Paper 4

1 Victorian
2 to keep her warm
3 the dining room
4 Helen
5–6 *They weren't allowed to talk and had to walk everywhere quietly. (lines 9–10)*
7–8 *Kate enjoyed learning how to bake bread because the cook was nice and allowed them to talk and laugh.*
9–11 *servants, folding napkins, bell in corridor, sweeping the floor with tea leaves*
12 bilingual   13 proclaim
14 biannual   15 pronoun
16 bicycle   17 prolonged
18 watch   19 plays
20 sweep   21 runs
22 win   23 swim
24 drops   25 root
26 night   27 adult
28 soldier   29 daisy
30 queue
31–36 A short passage that includes at least one full stop, two question marks, two exclamation marks and a pair of brackets.
37–43 (There are only grey squirrels in Britain.)
   <u>Flying squirrels glide.</u>
   <u>Grey squirrels first came from America.</u>
   <u>Squirrels are found in Europe and elsewhere.</u>

A2

There are not many squirrels now.

A ground squirrel's home is called a tunnel.

Flying squirrels live in America only.

44 *huge*   **45** *gold*

46 *smart*   **47** *rickety*

48 *old*   **49** *fluffy*

50 puppy   **51** piglet

52 kitten   **53** foal

54 calf   **55** kid

56 duckling   **57** lamb

58 I'm never coming back./I'm not ever coming back.

59 Mark hasn't brought a towel for swimming.

60 The shopkeeper didn't have any fireworks.

61 There wasn't a teacher to help with my spelling./ There was no teacher to help with my spelling.

62 Amy hasn't a coat to wear./Amy has no coat to wear.

63 There weren't any goats on the farm./There were no goats on the farm.

64 attendant   **65** attendance

66 assistant   **67** assistance

68 confident   **69** confidence

70 correspondent   **71** correspondence

72 inexpensive   **73** impossible

74 unkind   **75** immature

76 imperfect   **77** undone

78 present   **79** future

80 present   **81** past

82 future   **83** past

84 The river broke its bank <u>and</u> many houses were flooded.

85 Dan cut himself, <u>however</u>, he didn't need a plaster.

86 Rani felt unwell, <u>nevertheless</u> she still went to school.

87 Harry agreed to go to the playground <u>though</u> he really wanted to go straight home.

88 Kim was given a prize <u>but</u> Henry has never won one.

89 The children weren't tired <u>although</u> it was past their bedtime.

90 far

91 under

92 bottom

93 out

94 night

95 cold

96–100 giraffe, vegetable, gem, page, magic

Paper 5

1 white

2 dry dusty grassland

3–4 tapir, zebra

5 lion

6 *Both animals feed either when the light is low (dusk or dawn) or during the night.*

7–8 *The Arctic fox is interesting because it changes its coat to camouflage itself with the seasons. '... the Arctic fox, who live in cold countries change the colour of their coats in winter so that the new white coat will tone in with the snow.'*

9 *a disguise*

10 *They don't need to hide from predators.*

11 church

12 class

13 bus

14 bush

15 box

16 waltz

17 atlas

18 *When making words plural that end in ch, sh, s, ss, x, z or zz add 'es' (but remember there are always exceptions to the rule).*

19–20 <u>Mine</u> is smaller than <u>yours</u>.

21–22 <u>I</u> am glad <u>they</u> have bought a dog.

23–24 <u>You</u> need to buy <u>him</u> a present.

25–26 Have <u>you</u> taken <u>mine</u>?

27–28 <u>We</u> have put <u>ours</u> over there.

29–31 **J**ason **S**aves the **D**ay

32–34 **T**he **H**istory of the **V**ikings

35–38 **F**ootball **S**kills **M**ade **F**un

39 *leave*

40 *brave*

41 *enough*

42 *asked*

43 *whole*

44 *scattered*

45 *met, faced*

46 Where's your basket?

47 Isn't it over there?

48 You'll do it soon.

49 We shan't do that!

50 I won't open the door.

51 We should've let her play with us.

52 We'll have to go next time.

53 Northallerton

54 Northampton

55 Northwich

56 Norwich

57 Norwood

58 Nottingham

59–63 Five sentences completed with the addition of a relative clause, e.g. The horse that I rode came last.

64 laughable   **65** responsible

66 reasonable   **67** combustible

68 accessible   **69** adorable

70 considerable   **71** sensible

72 down   **73** behind

74 through   **75** behind

76 in   **77** on

78 down   **79** among

80 false   **81** true

82 true   **83** true

84 true   **85** true

86 *bear*   **87** *height*

88 *enough*   **89** *have*

90 *dive*   **91** *tow*

92 *e.g. stumbled*

93–94 *screamed, leap*

95 *wandered*

96 *shuddered*

97–100 *podcast, hippy, television, grunge, software, docudrama, nerd, jukebox, reggae, website, dotcom, clone*

Paper 6

1 hill
2 to see what is making the noise
3 ones with no lights
4–6 cheques, postal orders, letters
7 *As the train moves forward the steam makes a trail over the shoulder of the train.*
8 *goes down*
9 *Tall chimney stacks facing each other in rows*
10 'But a jug in a bedroom gently shakes' (line 16)
11 <u>pressu</u>re
12 <u>detect</u>ive
13 <u>black</u>en
14 re<u>cover</u>ed
15 <u>sign</u>ature
16 <u>fresh</u>ly
17 <u>swim</u>ming
18 un<u>help</u>ful
19 we
20 play
21 sad
22 quickly
23 aunt
24 it
25 teach
26 lesson
27 groan
28 board
29 lone
30 stakes
31 to
32 hour
33 proper
34 collective
35 common
36 abstract
37 collective
38 proper
39 abstract
40 to be hard up – to be short of money
41 to get into hot water – to get into trouble
42 to have forty winks – to have a short sleep
43 to go on all fours – to crawl on hands and knees
44 to play with fire – to ask for trouble
45 to face the music – to take punishment without complaint
46 to lead a dog's life – to be treated badly
47 *although*
48 *since*
49 *until*
50 *but*
51 *because*
52 *so*
53 *and*
54 burglary
55 confectionery
56 jewellery
57 momentary
58 slippery
59 dictionary
60 shrubbery
61 boundary
62 was
63 are
64 is
65 were
66 are
67 was
68–71 "Can I have some of your drink?" asked Karen.
72–78 "Are you up yet?" Jake's mum called. "It is time for school."
79 phone
80 cycle or bike
81 exam
82 photo
83 hippo
84 maths
85 *Nelson and his ship, the* Victory
86 Richard Edmunds
87 Friday and Saturday
88 *It will give them information about the historic ship moored at their city.*
89 Child's own heading showing evidence s/he has thought about what might attract the reader to read the article, e.g. *Barncroft Primary School to do Nelson's Adventure.*
90 *co-operate*
91 *re-enter*
92 *bi-monthly*
93 *cross-reference*
94 *de-ice*
95 *ex-directory*
96 She will take a photo.
97 I will/shall wake up at 7 o'clock.
98 I will/shall enjoy that piece of cake.
99 It will rain/It will be raining.
100 We will play on the swings.

Paper 7

1 It would give him food for three days.
2 rushed along shouting
3–4 the hyena, smaller wild animals
5 *They would quickly finish the meat he had found.*
6 *No, he made it up to get rid of his children.*
7 *As animals heard the news they told friends and family and the message spread.*
8–9 *So many animals passed him on the way to the village that eventually the hyena thought that maybe he had been right and therefore headed to the village to find all the dead asses.* Evidence from passage needed to support answer, e.g. *'Well, he said to himself, it looks as if it must be true.'*
10 basement
11 happiness
12 argument
13 spiteful
14 useful
15 loneliness
16 The <u>hollow-eyed, pale-faced</u> mask frightened the children.

17 The <u>huge, mottled brown</u> horse bounded about the field.

18 Snow fell from the <u>twisted, broken</u> branch.

19 The <u>cold and fresh</u> water tasted lovely.

20 George put on his <u>warm, cosy</u> jumper.

21 The <u>long, smooth</u> snake hid under the rock for protection.

22 pasta – Italy

23 boomerang – Australia

24 wok – China

25 restaurant – France

26 moose – America

27 pyjamas – India

28 *quietly*

29 *angrily*

30 *loudly*

31 *well*

32 *softly*

33 *smugly*

34 *heartily*

35 *sternly*

36 Mark suddenly jumped, the dog having caught him unawares.

37–38 Time and time again, as the boat was tossed by the waves, the helicopter crew tried to save the fishermen.

39–40 The shop, which earlier had been bustling with shoppers, was now quiet.

41–42 Susie and Tariq, already soaked from the pouring rain, ran to find cover.

43–44 richer richest

45–46 worse worst

47–48 quieter quietest

49–50 prettier prettiest

51–52 more most

53–54 earlier earliest

55 fork

56 fortnight

57 doorbell or knocker

58 recite or recount

59 puppet or marionette

60 stem or stalk

61 stage

62 string

63 halves

64 shelves

65 thieves

66 leaves

67 knives

68 calves

69–87 "Quick!" shouted Nina. "The water will trap us in the cave if we don't hurry."
"I know!" screamed James trying to be heard above the thundering waves. As James ran, his feet barely touched the ground.

88 pizza

89 volcano

90 piano

91 umbrella

92 Italy

93 *ordinary* or *unattractive* or *simple*

94 *pull* or *drag*

95 *force* or *persuade* or *poke* or *press*

96 pull

97–98 is, are

99 was

100 were

Paper 8

1 Toad talks too much

2 Thursday

3–4 *He doesn't think very highly of them. He shows this when he says that he has several aunts who ought to be washerwomen.*

5–6 *I would have felt angry because I was trying to help and he was being rude about my aunt.*

7 *Some words are put into italics to highlight the strength of feeling/importance that they hold in the text.*

8–10 *horrid – for speaking in an unflattering way about her aunt*
proud – not willing to be seen as a washerwoman
ungrateful – for his reaction to her suggestion

11–12 *The washerwoman demanded that she should be bound, gagged and dumped in a corner. This was to help persuade the guards that she had nothing to do with Toad's escape.*

13–14 *pretty attractive*

15–16 *wrong incorrect*

17–18 *happy amused*

19–20 *mean unkind*

21–22 *shout yell*

23 did

24 was

25 are

26 were

27 have

28 shall

29 has

30 will

31 dramatise

32 solidify

33 magnetise or magnify

34 thicken

35 terrorise or terrify

36 weaken

37 blacken

38 fertilise

39 *fought*

40 *borough*

41 *enough*

42 *bough*

43 *dough*

44–47 "When can we go swimming?" asked Jenny.

48–51 "We will be late!" Mum yelled.

52 where

53 because

54 although

55 which

56 there

57 They're

58 their
59 there
60–61 their, their
62 They're
63–64 their, there
65 km
66 UK
67 CD
68 MP
69 USA
70 TV
71 Dr
72 anything
73 nothing
74 anything
75 anything
76 nothing
77 nothing
78 Ben asked where his bag was.
79 Dad said we needed to be quick.
80 The children asked whether they could go to the fair.
81 The teacher explained that they were going to bake a cake.
82 *empty*
83 *hung*
84 *vain/proud*
85 *finished*
86 *cruelly*
87 *understood*
88 noun
89 noun
90 noun
91 verb
92 verb
93 verb
94 false
95 don't know
96 false
97 true
98 false
99 false
100 true

Paper 9

1 sunny
2–3 a farmer, me
4 *And gurgled awhile.*
5 *in the refreshment room*
6 *The last part of the journey home.*
7–8 The family have been to the sea, as indicated in line 12 'And the salt on my face, not of tears, not tears, but the sea.'
9–10 *As you read the poem the pace gets faster. The poet is trying to convey the speed of the train through the words he uses.*
11–12 *When there is driving rain often images become blurred, the poet is suggesting that the speed of the train is having the same effect.*
13–15 *faster (line 1), charging (line 3), fly (line 6)*
16 flies
17 bullies
18 valleys
19 journeys
20 ladies
21 hobbies
22 cries
23 donkeys
24 up
25 with

26 from
27 over or up
28 behind
29 on or behind
30 Rosie's knitting was finished at last.
31 Tony's dog ran away last week.
32 The two boys' football went over the fence.
33 The three rabbits' hutches fell down in the wind.
34 Caroline's leg hurt after she slipped on the ice.
35 My mother's bedroom was a mess.
36 *fight*
37 *dove*
38 *ridge*
39 *full*
40 *toast*
41 *more*
42 *strange*
43 *stitch*

44–52

	er	est	ish
long	longer	longest	longish
small	smaller	smallest	smallish
late	later	latest	latish

53 nowt – nothing
54 scoff – eat
55 wee – little
56 aye – yes
57 bairn – child
58 tatties – potatoes
59 skullache – headache
60–62 The candles blew out, plunging the children into darkness.
63–65 Carrying piles of apples, the carts were pulled down the road.
66–68 High in the sky, the birds were feeding on the flying insects.
69 UN
70 BBC
71 RAF
72 NATO
73 JP
74 HGV
75 CID
76–87 **Nouns**: rabbit, cave, food, rock, remains, turnip, search
Adjectives: small, weak, mouldy
Verbs: searched, looking, could, find, were, sighed, continued
Adverbs: frantically, loudly
Prepositions: in, for, behind, of
Conjunctions: but, and
88–91 four words with a silent letter, e.g. *write, raspberry, psalm, scissors*
92 He/She strokes the dog.
93 He/She cries loudly.
94 He/She washes his/her hair.
95 He/She cooks a meal.
96 drake
97 actor
98 prince
99 hero
100 landlord

Paper 10

1 night-time
2 as sharp as a knife
3 into her bed
4–5 *the look of the devil, frightening*
   bending low, holding arms and legs together tightly
6 *She was so scared she couldn't produce a sound.*
7–8 *enormous, long, pale, wrinkly (lines 26–27)*
9–10 'If you can think of anything more terrifying than that happening to you in the middle of the night, then let's hear about it.' *The author communicates with the reader like this to encourage us to think about just how scary the situation for Sophie is.*
11–12 *He is very large with a long, pale, wrinkly face. He has bright, flashing eyes, huge ears, a sharp nose, strong fingers, arms as thick as tree trunks and huge hands.*
13–15 The child's description of how Sophie felt, being carried from her bed by the Giant. Reference needs to be made to specific lines/phrases from the passage, e.g. *I think Sophie was terrified, because she 'knew exactly what was going on although she couldn't see it happening.' Sophie was imprisoned in her bedclothes and taken away by the Giant.*
16 shyly
17 spied
18 tried
19 easier
20 drying
21 cried
22–31 **S**uddenly, out of the tunnel emerged the **F**lying **S**cotsman. **H**annah and **L**eroy had been waiting for this moment, ever since reading about this train in **F**amous **T**rains of the **P**ast. **T**hey screamed with excitement as it flew past them on its way to **B**anbury.
32–33 *everyone everything*
34–35 *candlelight candlestick*
36–37 *rainbow raindrop*
38–39 *playtime playground*
40–42 Each of the listed adverbs written in a different sentence e.g. *Barney shouted angrily at the bullies.*

43–54

Common nouns	Proper nouns	Collective nouns	Abstract nouns
door	France	team	love
leg	Nigel	bunch	sympathy
camel	Hyde Park	swarm	justice

55 official
56 confidential
57 essential
58 commercial
59 artificial
60 partial
61–64 Adjectival phrases added in the gaps of sentences e.g. *Tola slept peacefully in her cosy, warm bed.*
65 *deactivate*
66 *rejoin*
67 *mistreat*
68 *disembark*
69 *discontinue*
70 *redefine*
71 *decompose*
72 *overhead*
73 x
74 ✓
75 ✓
76 x
77 x
78 ✓
79 x
80–81 **Aden ran with all his might** when he saw the raging bull.
82–83 **Julie combed her hair constantly** because she wanted straight hair.
84–85 **While Yan was painting a picture,** the lights suddenly went off.
86–91 Three sentences indicating parenthesis, each using brackets, dashes or commas.
92–94 *whoosh, bang, zoom*
95–97 *plip plop, squelch, splash*
98–100 *moo, crunch, squeak*

Paper 11

1 disappear quickly and quietly
2 people
3 brown
4 *It enables them to hear people a mile away.*
5–6 *Their feet grow natural leather soles and they are covered in thick warm brown hair.*
7 '... laugh deep fruity laughs (especially after dinner which they have twice a day when they can get it).'
8 *kind-looking face*
9–11 *Hobbits are half the size; Hobbits aren't stupid like the Big People; Hobbits have feet that grow natural leather soles and thick warm brown hair.*
12–14 *I think that the Big People are frightening because they are twice as tall as we are so when they come near, I run away and hide. They are also quite stupid because they walk so heavily that we know they are coming.*
15–23 diner, dinner, bath, bathe, sit, thorough, pasted, lung, lunge
24 sky
25 life
26 lorry
27 giraffe
28 ox
29 posy
30–35 Three sentences, each sentence including two possessive pronouns underlined, e.g. *Our rabbit is bigger than his.*
36 *but*
37 *but*
38 *until*
39 *when*
40 *and*
41 *but/although*
42 telephone
43 automotive

44 circumnavigate
45 biplane
46 television
47 autobiography
48 telescope
49 bifocals
50–67 **Nouns**: coffee, horror, scoundrel
Verbs: jumped, threw, going
Adjectives: strange, curly, thin
Adverbs: truly, really, almost
Prepositions: of, into, with
Pronouns: it, himself, you
68–69 were   was
70 were
71–72 were   was
73 was
74 head
75 blanket
76 leaf
77 seat
78 horse
79 rat
80 fence
81–84 Amusing sentences containing the given preposition
e.g. *It was only after leaning against the fence that
Josh realised it had just been painted.*
85–92

France	Spain	Italy
café	tortilla	gondola
boutique	mosquito	macaroni
adieu	armadillo	opera

93 we'll
94 they'll
95 shouldn't
96 I've
97 hasn't
98 won't
99 there's
100 you're

Paper 12

1 India
2 people
3 six hundred years ago
4 *as hard as he could*
5–6 *'The king trembled at the thought of the snake-
god's anger – would he bring fire and plague to his
subjects, or even destroy the world?'*
7 *gifts*
8–9 *I would have felt upset because I had just put my
kingdom and all of my subjects in danger.*
10–11 *no more war and unrest*
12 imperfect
13 incorrect
14 inaccurate
15 impure
16 imbalance
17 incomplete
18 impatient
19 invisible
20 Mum called that it was time for dinner.
21 The children asked if they could go out to play.
22 David whispered to Amie that he was hiding in the
shed.
23 The postman mumbled that it was really cold today.
24 Gina exclaimed that she loved her new shoes.
25 *crackle*
26 *gasp, pant*
27 *squelch*
28 *thump*
29 *slam*
30 *splash*
31 *beep, beep*
32 fitted
33 carried
34 knotted
35 picked
36 married
37 hunted
38 *Tom ate his food because he was very hungry.*
39 *The sun shone brightly and woke Gemma up.*
40 *The school trip was great fun and they didn't want to
go home.*
41 *Nasar learnt his spelling homework but he still got
some wrong in the test.*
42 past   42 past
44 present   45 present
46 future   47 past
48 future
49–60 **Nouns**: beauty bread
Adjectives: silky fluffy
Verbs: stumbled heaved
Adverbs: frantically stupidly
Prepositions: of among
Conjunctions: because although
61 *tried*   62 *asked*
63 *said*   64 *stuck*
65 *often*   66 *given*
67 *rich*   68 *clapped*
69 attract   70 entertain
71 depart   72 attach
73 fail   74 complete
75 away   76 clock
77 makes   78 fill
79 drain   80 stair
81 same
82 I haven't got any money./I have no money.
83 There wasn't a clown at the circus./There were no
clowns at the circus.
84 There weren't any sweets in the jar./There were no
sweets in the jar.
85 Tina hasn't got an umbrella for the rain./Tina has no
umbrella for the rain./Tina doesn't have an umbrella
for the rain.
86–100 "Quick, come here!" called Tom.
The rain was falling heavily and they wanted to avoid
getting wet.
"When do you think it will stop?" asked Misha.